BATHING SPACES

DESIGNS FOR PAMPERING BODY AND SOUL

ALI HANAN

ROCKPORT PUBLISHERS

Acknowledgments

When most of you flick through this book in your freshly poured hot tub, please remember that behind it there's been a whole team of people: the inspirational, warm-humoured, patient, enthusiastic (the list of adjectives could go on and on here) team at Rockport (particularly Martha Wetherill, for her "keep the faith" emails and this wonderful opportunity; Stephen Perfetto for his sharp design eye; Jay Donahue for his understanding; Kiana Cassidy for helping me out; and of course Francine Hornberger for her guidance and direction in shaping the book). And another thanks too to the funny, clever Katie Ebben from *ELLE Decoration* who put us in touch. Plus a special thanks to The Hempel Hotel. Oh, and thanks to all the photographers and picture researchers for their breath-taking images, particularly Mike Paul (and Kimiko). And thanks to my personal team: Dame Liz, Murray Hanan and Dizz.

First published in the United States of America by
Rockport Publishers, Inc.
33 Commercial Street
Gloucester, Massachusetts 01930-5089
Telephone: (978) 282-9590
Facsimile: (978) 283-2742
www.rockpub.com

ISBN 1-56496-717-4

10 9 8 7 6 5 4 3 2

Photo Editor & Art Direction: Stephen Perfetto
Design: Terry Patton Rhoads
Cover Image: Jake Fitzjones

Printed in China.

contents

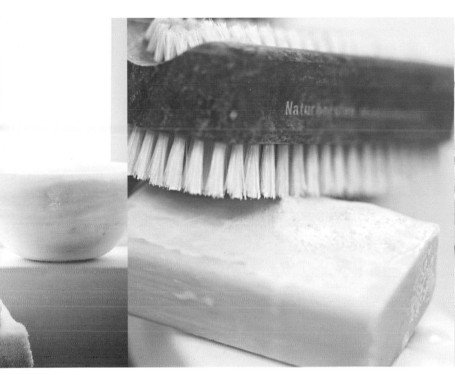

In Harmony With Nature

Design in harmony with the environment

Exotic Soaks

Uncommon, ingenious designs for health and relaxation

introduction
the art of bathing

THERE IS NOTHING QUITE LIKE SOAKING IN A BATH. Imagine it. The feeling of bliss and well-being as you sink into a hot, steamy tub. And, once immersed, the sensuous feeling of silky water on your skin. In a lifetime, the average person will spend as much as three years washing his or her body. So why not make the ritual of bathing one to celebrate, and turn it into a sensual, pleasurable, indulgent, luxurious experience?

Bathing appeals to an innate human need. Water, in most cultures, is linked with spiritual activities and sacred ceremonies. The Chinese, for example, believe running water embodies chi, the force that drives life itself. The sound of flowing water calms and soothes jangled nerves. Psychoanalysts connect our passion for water back to the womb. Somehow, deep within our psyche, sinking our bodies into a bath replicates a memory of a place where we felt safe, nurtured, and protected. The hug of water is like a maternal embrace.

Bathing serves the intellect as well. While once Archimedes shouted "Eureka!" (and discovered the formula of fluid displacement), today, one of America's most powerful men, Alan Greenspan, spends two hours a day in his "working bath," solving the problems of the U.S. economy. When the body is weightless, the mind, liberated and recharged, is free to think.

If bathing is the art, then the bathroom is the gallery. All too often, the bathroom is an afterthought, relegated to the smallest, darkest room in the home—a throwback to the prudish Victorians who viewed bathing as a clinical undertaking performed in the name of hygiene and sanitation. But now the bathroom is stepping out of its closet. People have begun to forego spare bedrooms, converting attics and basements, and building bathrooms into conservatories. The bathroom is, finally, receiving the space it deserves.

Plus, the bathroom has received a designer makeover. Responding to the desire for contemporary bathroom style, manufacturers have taken the plunge and are commissioning coveted bathroom ware. Designer Philippe Starck's ground-breaking designs have inspired a new wave of designers and architects to revamp the traditional tub. Now cutting-edge bathroom design is making the bathroom too chic to languish behind locked doors.

Large bathrooms are becoming second living rooms. Fast paced lifestyles demand a room that's a relaxing retreat to lounge, socialize, exercise, or mediate. Whether a Zen-like retreat or a living room complete with day beds, yoga mats and stacks of magazines, the bathroom has become the home's sanctuary, a space dedicated to peace, calm, and repose. While the kitchen might be the heart of the home, the bathroom is its soul

Whether you're redesigning an old bathroom or renovating a new one, make the bathroom's role in your home a prestigious one. Be inspired by the pages in this book. Pour a fragrant bath to its brim and take *Bathing Spaces* with you. After all, there's nothing like a good book to read while reveling in a long, hot soak.

traditional havens

WHEN WE IMMERSE OUR BODIES IN A HOT BATH,

WE CELEBRATE A TIME-HONORED RITUAL.

In Japanese culture, the bath is a place to find outer cleanliness and inner peace. Nature is an integral part of the experience.

The rite of bathing reflects our special relationship with water, an element that early on acts as our only connection to the world. The warm, maternal comfort of water soothes and cleanses our bodies and placates and calms our souls.

Today's bathing spaces descend directly from past traditions. The Californian hot tub, for example, has its roots in the Japanese *onsen,* an outdoor communal bath. The mosaic-tiled Arabic *hamam,* where daybeds and bathing areas mix together, has been the impetus behind the new "wet living room" concept. The Scandinavian sauna is de rigueur for homes in cold climates. And our penchant for generous bath tubs stems from the Victorian taste for large *bateau* baths.

"Americans bathe to get clean, the Japanese clean to bathe," as someone once noted. To the Japanese, the bath is a space for repose and contemplation. The work of washing and scrubbing the body is done *before* stepping into the *furo* (a private bath); the Japanese consider the Western habit of cleansing and soaking in the same tub unhygienic and disagreeable. In the Japanese bath-room, visual (and therefore mental) clutter is eschewed by paring back objects in the bath and keeping it simple.

While bathing is a private affair in Western culture, in the Arab world bathing is a communal experience. Whereas the idea of a "wet living room" is just emerg-ing in Western space, the *hamam,* a place also for repose and spiritual contem-plation, acts as the community's fulcrum—people come to socialize as much to bathe. After washing, bathers recline on daybeds and chat, doze, or read.

Finns are known to build their sauna before building their house. There are over two million of these sweat lodges in Finland, a huge number considering there are only five million Finns. The wood-lined, airtight structure centers on a stove where water is poured on top of hot coals to create steam to heat up the cabin and the bather. After sweating out toxins, bathers plunge into cold pools to close up the skin's opened pores and stimulate the body's nervous system.

Old Victorian styles are now hot modern favorites. Bathing in the Victorian era meant heating up buckets of water, so it was commonplace to wash in front of the fire in the living room, or even for a whole family to share one bath. Baths with clawed feet in front of fireplaces pay homage to this era.

Such bathing customs sound appealing, but what are the best ways to integrate these ideas into a modern bathing space? Take from each tradition a favorite activity, design, or theme. To emulate Japanese philosophy, install a separate shower for washing; keep the bath strictly for relaxing. The Japanese often employ a low-level wooden stool in the shower room to enable the lower body to be scrubbed without backache—also handy for the elderly or for perching on while washing children.

Bathe with nature in view—another element of the Japanese tradition to covet. Expand windows to contemplate natural vistas, or if your room is windowless, collect driftwood, pebbles, or seashells, and make a display to reconnect with the natural world.

A recent trend in design stemming from Japanese tradition is soaking in a wooden bath. Sensuous to the touch and pungently aromatic when wet, wooden tubs also have antibacterial properties. Choose a sustainable or recycled hardwood, such as *iroko*, cedar, or *merabau;* and ask a cabinetmaker or specialist to tailor one to your bathroom.

To recreate a *hamam*-like atmosphere, allow space for a luxurious daybed to recline on. Keep plenty of towels, a bathrobe, and slippers close at hand to prevent chills. Thrill the soles of your feet with another *hamam* idea, underfloor heating, invented by the Romans in A.D. 60. Best installed at the building stage, the most common system (a wet system) involves hot water piped underneath the floor, running off a central heating system; electric underfloor systems are also available.

Saunas are snug pinewood log cabins built around a wood or electric stove. Bathers splash water over hot coals to create steam, often scented with eucalyptus oils. In Scandinavian culture, no heated conversations are permitted within the sauna's confines; it is a place for physical and mental rejuvenation only. To build, seek advice from a specialist. Otherwise just go for the look and apply wood cladding to the walls, emulating its soft, natural look.

To hark back to Victorian times, source imitation French-*bateau* designs or head to architectural salvage yards and buy the real thing. Costs for refiring and reenameling baths can add up, however, so check out waste traps and plumbing requirements before you take the financial plunge.

A wooden tub, Japanese style, provides a sit-up bath. In Japanese culture, the body is thoroughly scrubbed and cleansed before bathing. A small stool and hand-shower enables the bather to thoroughly cleanse themselves.

Above: Pine wood cladding in this bathroom harks back to a Scandinavian sauna.

Opposite: Double sinks are a practical idea for busy households. Here the sinks are designed to look like part of a large dresser, with ample storage underneath.

FENG SHUI
FOR THE BATH

ACCORDING TO FENG SHUI, WHEN WATER FLOWS OUT OF THE HOUSE IT TAKES CRUCIAL CHI, OR LIFE ENERGY, WITH IT. BATHROOMS, THEREFORE, SAP A HOUSE'S ENERGY. TO COUNTERBALANCE THIS OUTFLOW, CREATE UPWARD ENERGY BY GROWING PLANTS IN THE BATHROOM. AND TO CONTAIN ENERGY, ALWAYS KEEP THE TOILET BOWL LID CLOSED. AS THE BATHROOM IS USUALLY THE FIRST PLACE YOU'LL VISIT DURING THE DAY, FENG SHUI RECOMMENDS ADDING SOMETHING THAT WILL MAKE YOU LAUGH OR SMILE TO START THE DAY OUT ON A HIGH NOTE.

Opposite: Saunas are a luxurious addition to any home. The minimum size is 39 inches by 39 inches by 7 feet (1 m x 1 m x 2 m), so saunas can be squeezed into basements, under stairwells, or installed outdoors in a shed.

Above: Start your day with a smile, and balance the energy-draining effect of plumbing with plants.

Inside a traditional Lebanese private bathroom, Romanesque arches, an octagonal bath, and shafts of natural light punctuate the space. Couches positioned on a platform under the windows reinforce the idea of bathing space as relaxation haven.

a **sofa** in the bathroom

ALTHOUGH THE KITCHEN HAS BEEN TOUTED AS THE NEW LIVING ROOM, CONSIDER THE BATH-ROOM, A PLACE DEDICATED TO RELAXATION AND REPOSE VERSUS THE FUNCTION AND ACTIVITY OF THE KITCHEN, INSTEAD. WHERE WOULD YOU RATHER HANG OUT?

- Locate your bathroom in the largest space possible. Don't condemn the bathroom to a small, dark room. Find space in your home by converting a spare bedroom, using a neglected loft, or adding a conservatory.

- Furnish with a sofa or daybed. A lounger is essential for post-bath reclining, beauty treatments, and visitors.

- Install a TV or stereo. Before you purchase electrical equipment, find out what your local regulations are as some countries forbid main sockets in wet areas. Equipment outside the room, however, can be connected to speakers within so bathers can relax to ambient sounds. Consult an electrician.

- Keep lighting levels flexible. Install a dimmer switch for mellow moods.

- Go hotel—turn the whole room into a "wet" living area. Make the room watertight so you can splash freely. Cover floors and walls in tile and run water into a central drainage system.

A sense of space, a place to be at liberty to lounge around and read a book— whether in the tub or on the sofa—or curl up for a catnap. These are the ingredients that make a bathroom indulgent.

An extra ledge in a bathroom, here formed under a deep-set window, can be used for
bathroom necessities such as a stack of linens or to create a vignette of pretty objects to
gaze upon while in the bath.

Victorian families used to bathe together in front of fireplaces where large pots of water were heated on the flames. The fireplace as the focal point of this room recalls those times.

Above: Crisp, fresh white towels imbue a bathing space with a feeling of freshness and cleanliness.

Right: Bath and shower curtains add a splash of romance, but their purpose is grounded in practicality: in addition to protecting the bathroom floor from water damage, they retain and economize on heat and hold in steam, essential for soft, exfoliated skin.

This page, top: Soaking in the bath might be one of the few times of the day that you have time to yourself. Place a magazine rack within reach and read all those articles you haven't had time for.

This page, bottom: At one time, bathrooms were relegated to dark, pint-sized, back rooms. Now, they've become bright, expansive spaces and are given as much design attention as public areas of the home. Here, a duck-egg blue freestanding tub resting on a terra-cotta tiled floor dominates a bright, airy room.

Opposite: Good old-fashioned furniture and bath fittings—large pillar taps and spouts—create more of an atmosphere than their mass-produced counterparts.

A simple cream bathroom with a compelling visual shock: a bright red bath that beckons like a beacon.

Above: A bateau bath has a beautiful, sculptural shape. A large window makes its silhouetted shape look even more inviting.

Opposite: A tranquil haven. Throughout time, bathing has been a ritual that goes beyond cleaning the body. A smooth, cool limestone floor adds to the ambience.

the **bathroom**-cum-**dressing** room

THROUGHOUT THE CENTURIES, BATHROOMS HAVE BEEN ALSO USED AS DRESSING ROOMS. THE TRADITION OF MIXING DRESSING AND BATHING AREAS MAKES PERFECT SENSE. INSTEAD OF WRAPPING YOURSELF IN A BATHROBE TO TRAIPSE TO THE NEXT ROOM TO GET DRESSED, WHY NOT KEEP CLOTHES CLOSE AT HAND—IN THE BATHROOM?

• Add an en suite. Divide your master bedroom in two and incorporate a bathroom into one half. Use the dividing panel between rooms as a storage wall for clothes.

• Put a bath in your bedroom. Instead of adding an en suite, save space by siting a tub in your boudoir.

• Store clothes in the bathroom. Or keep the bedroom strictly for sleeping, and make the bathroom into a dressing room. Hang shirts on rails, put underwear in nearby drawer units, and build-in wardrobes.

• Invest in a dressing table and stool. Dressers are making a comeback as a way of dedicating an area to lotions, toiletries, and makeup. Ensure dresser mirrors are well lit. Place lights on either side of the mirror rather than over-head (otherwise Dracula-like shadows will be cast over your face).

With no boundaries between bathroom and bedroom, there is the luxury of one huge space. Stumble out of the bath, and relaxed, step straight into bed; or stumble out of bed, refresh yourself in a quick cool bath, and be ready to face the day.

design secrets

THE MODERN BATHROOM IS DESIGNED FOR

PHYSICAL, MENTAL, AND EMOTIONAL RENEWAL;

THEREFORE, ITS DECOR SHOULD ENTICE YOU TO SPEND TIME THERE.

The bathroom blends seamlessly into this open plan space. For privacy, simply slide the doors closed.

The bath is the invitation, but the rest of the room is the main event. The secrets of good design lie in putting down functional foundations. So where to start?

If you're designing a bath from scratch in an existing space, think of the room in relation to the rest of the house. Remember that a bath doesn't have to be confined to the bathroom. Size and shape isn't a limitation, either, as manufacturers now produce a number of tailored bathtub models that squeeze into capsule-sized and awkwardly shaped bathrooms.

When planning a bathroom, the real key to success is to define its role in the house. Distilling what you need it for is an essential part of the planning process. Will you use it as a dressing room, exercise area, or socializing space? Is it going to be a busy family hub? Would double sinks alleviate congestion at peak times? Is it possible to have a separate room for the toilet? Be honest about who will use the bath and why, how often, and what you most want from it.

Next, work out the utilities you want and need in the space. Would you like a bidet; a hand-held or a wall-mounted shower; a sit-up bath? Selecting fixtures and fittings is vital—they must stand the test of time, both in function and style. To garner an idea of a workable layout, take a sheet of graph paper and mark the dimensions of your bathroom (bird's-eye view), then cut out proposed fittings. Juggle them around to see how they will work, keeping in mind existing or proposed plumbing and the need to allow for room to move around.

Once the bathroom's purpose is clearly defined, the nuts and bolts—plumbing and electrical requirements—need to be considered. Regulations vary so seek the advice of a professional to learn about the regulations in your area. Drainage pipes, local plumbing regulations, electrical outlets, and ventilation systems must also comply with local health and safety regulations. At this stage, plan lighting and heating systems. Make sure these are installed properly as alterations at a later stage are disruptive and costly.

The floor must be nonslip, easy to clean, resistant to excessive amounts of moisture, and gentle on bare feet. Where splashes are kept to a minimum (in an adult en suite, for example) bathroom-quality carpet (rubber-backed and made of cotton or synthetic fibers) is sensuous underfoot. While traditional coverings such as vinyl, rubber, and linoleum are all relatively inexpensive to buy and put down, nothing endures as well as marble, slate, and granite. With tiles, opt for nonglazed, nonslip varieties, and install underfloor heating to take away the chill. Wooden flooring is prone to rot when exposed to excessive moisture, so if this is your choice, protect it with a wax or sealant to increase its longevity.

Walls in a bathroom are functional as well as aesthetic. They must be able to counteract the adverse effects of water and steam. To protect against dampness, seal the areas around the bath, basin, and shower with materials like Perspex, tiles, polished steel, mirrors, sealed tongue and groove, and glass or other similar water-repellent materials. Nothing beats paint to simply transform walls. Look for bathroom-friendly, antifungal varieties, and try unusual paint effects such as sponging or trompe l'oeil to add visual interest.

Really focus on style. Rip out ideas from magazines, plunder inspirations from friend's houses, or let finds such as fittings and furniture direct you to a style that suits you. Something as simple as a Victorian pillar tap might spark off a traditional classic look or equivocally, a sleek, stainless-steel fitting might trigger an industrial hi-tech look. Let your imagination roam.

The wall between bathroom and bedroom is made up of an opaque glass, which allows for light to filter into the bathroom without compromising privacy.

Bathing and dressing were, at one time, integrated activities.

The modern take on this old tradition is the en suite.

Tiny, white mosaic tiles decorate the floor for a practical wet area, while blue tiles decorate the sides of the hand basin and tub. A sliding door separates bathroom from bedroom.

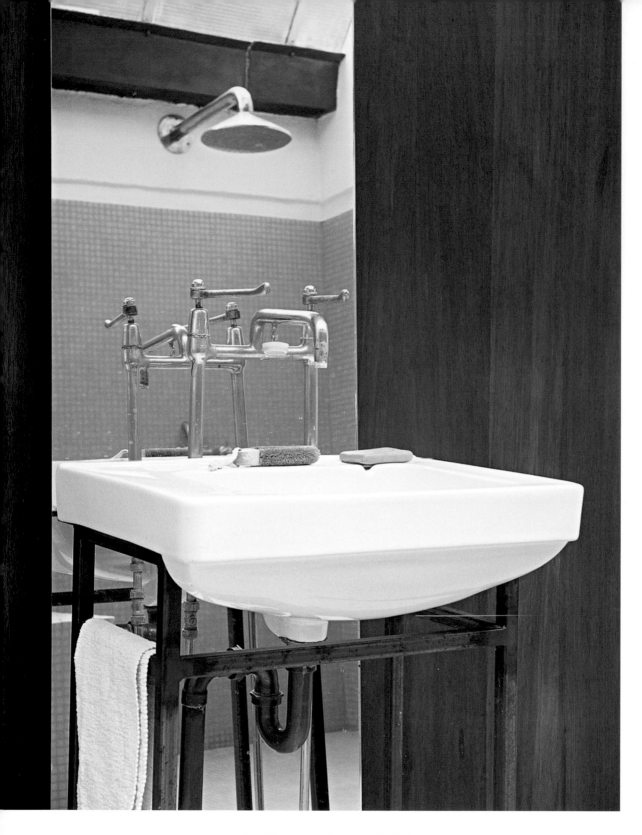

From the bedroom (opposite), the bathroom in this London loft looks bewitchingly
inviting. The tap fittings on the elegant,
freestanding sink (above) originally came
from an old demolished hospital.

small-**space** solutions

IS YOUR BATHROOM BARELY LARGE ENOUGH TO SWING A TOWEL IN? DON'T DESPAIR, THERE ARE A NUMBER OF CLEVER WAYS TO MAKE SMALL SPACES APPEAR LARGER.

- Use corner or wall-hung furnishings and fixtures. Wall-hung fixtures, such as basins, bidets, and toilets, make a room seem more spacious because they free up floor space. Wall-mounted taps and spouts also save precious inches, and corner sinks and toilets give a neat, "tucked-away" appearance.

- Use lighting to create optical illusions. Lighting tricks, such as placing spotlights around the perimeter of the ceiling, enlarge a space. Create a feeling of expansion by using mirrors to bounce light around the room.

- Create visual continuity with color. Use a monochrome pale color (pale colors are expansive, while dark colors recede) to visually enlarge rooms.

- Create different floor levels. Differing levels add new spatial dimensions. If creating a step up to a bath, use the storage space underneath the step for accessories.

- Opt for clean lines and minimalist styling. Go Zen. A bathroom really needs very little out in the open. The more you tuck away behind closed doors, the more uncluttered visual space you create.

A sliding mirror acts as a wall divider between the bathroom and bedroom. Having clothes close to the bath makes more ergonomic sense than traipsing around from bathroom to bedroom in a bathrobe.

Above: The bathroom has not been built into a room; rather, it stretches out along a corridor.

Opposite: Large, overhead skylights let in natural light. When the bather soaks in the tub, the view stretches out to infinity.

Far left and above: A terra-cotta red breathes life into this stylish bathroom. Don't confine glass shelves to the sink—store and display essential bath supplies, such as a scrubber and soap, on a glass perch close to a bath.

Middle: Instead of mounting the traditionally shaped bath on claw legs, the designer here has opted for a contemporary twist.

Left: Frosted glass sliding doors are an elegant solution to enclosing this small bath.

Opposite: Slide back the door to reveal well-lit, stylish bathroom. Mirrors help to make it brighter and larger.

Opposite: A glass wall provides an open-plan, non-confining space, while allowing light to flood the area. To keep proportions small in a confined bathing space, use mosaic tiles in muted, homogenous colors.

Above: Who said hand-basins had to be boring? Even the plumbing on this one is hip.

choosing a **bathtub**

STATISTICS SHOW THAT WHILE WE SPEND TWO-
THIRDS OF OUR LIVES IN BED, WE SPEND AT LEAST
THIRTY MONTHS IN THE BATH OR SHOWER. TAKE
TIME TO FIND A TUB THAT FITS LIKE A GLOVE.

- Try before you buy. Test out a bath by lying in it for at
  least ten minutes. Stretch your legs out, see if you like the
  positioning of the fittings (such as grab rails and taps),
  and check whether your neck is comfortably supported.

- Consider alternative shapes. Rectangular baths are popular
  because of their pragmatic shape. Round baths are good if
  bathing with children (though take more water to fill),
  while double-ended bateau baths with centered taps are
  great for bathing a deux. Square sit-up baths and corner
  baths are recommended for unusually shaped rooms or
  rooms with limited space.

- Think materials. Besides traditional ceramic or acrylic
  tubs, baths come in stainless steel, glass, copper, marble
  and wood—all sensuous, stylish options. Metal and marble
  baths don't retain the heat as well as their wood, acrylic,
  and ceramic cousins, so keep this in mind when you buy.

This unusual sub-level exclusive bathing space is made warm and inviting with
wood tones and white. The room is not ceilinged so the bather can soak up the
expansiveness of the space while soaking in the tub.

Opposite: To save space, taps are wall-mounted. This spout is generously large to ensure quick filling—perfect for rushed mornings.

Above: Two strip lights on either side of the mirror are the ideal way of providing lighting for shaving and applying make up as overhead lights sometimes cast brutal shadows. A large radiator beneath the sink blasts out heat into the room while also heating the water in the basin.

Following pages: White tiles are a practical choice. They're easy to clean, long lasting, and look timeless.

Opposite: Another angle of the same room shows the area to the left of the sink to be an unusual bathing space.

Above: Neutral tones and shiny surfaces keep this bathroom light and inviting. The passage between the shower and bath is open, allowing movement to flow freely between the areas as the bather cleanses the body ready to revel in the pleasures of the tub.

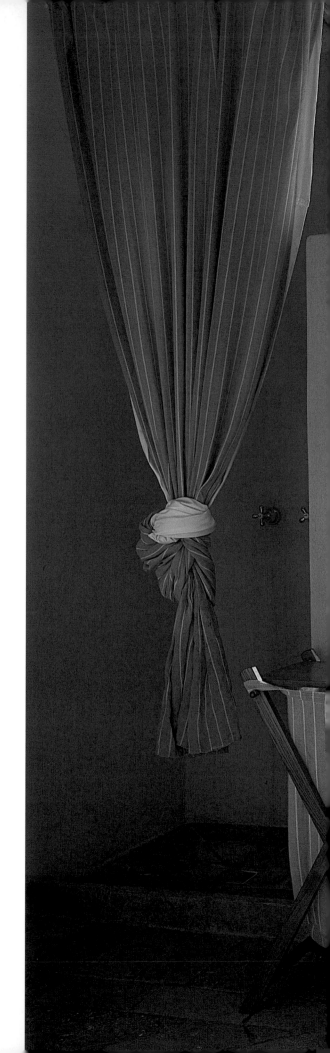

STOWAWAY

PLAN STORAGE SO YOU CAN STOW AWAY THE VISUALLY UNAPPEALING (LOTIONS, POTIONS, MEDICINES, TOWELS, CLEANSERS, TOILET PAPER). LEAVE OPEN SHELVING AND UNITS FOR OBJETS D'ART, FLOWERS, PEBBLES FROM THE BEACH, AND THINGS THAT YOU LOVE. STASH OTHER EXTRANEOUS BITS AWAY IN FREESTANDING UNITS, STORAGE CARTS, CONCEALED CABINETS, AND CABINETS UNDER THE SINK. TO CREATE MORE STORAGE SPACE, SQUARE OFF AWKWARDLY SHAPED ROOMS.

Right: Accessorize smartly. Here, a bath book stand is a nice design touch and makes sense for bathers who read while soaking—no more wet pages.

Above: Light from a window to the right of this view is reflected on the three-sided mirror, bouncing it back into the room in all directions. The wood of the mirror is picked up in the accessories: an innovative towel rack and a canvas folding hamper supported by a wooden frame.

relax and rejuvenate

JUST ENVISION ENTERING A ROOM WHERE THE DÉCOR MAKES YOU FEEL INSTANTLY

WARM, CALM, PAMPERED, AND RECHARGED.

Create a peaceful atmosphere by jux-taposing hard and soft, dark and light, rough and smooth. This bathroom, created by Anoushka Hempel, is the perfect example.

It is a room that makes you feel safe and comfortable. At its simplest, to enjoy a bath the bathroom must be clean, functional, and well heated. It doesn't take much to transform the room from utilitarian washroom to private retreat.

The easiest way to change a bathroom's atmosphere is to evoke a visual response. Color therapists extol that color is an emotional tonic. Pale colors emit vitality and light, while darker shades with heavy pigments reduce the amount of light reflected around a room, creating a sedate atmosphere. Temperate colors have a stimulating effect; cool ones create an atmosphere of relaxation. Each has a warm tone lurking within it: pale blue, for example, is cool, but royal blue is warm.

Unsurprisingly, bathrooms are often white, which is synonymous with cleanliness, purity, and space. However, white is also stark, cold, and clinical. Choose a color that appeals to you by painting large test blocks in the room and seeing how they vary with daylight. Live with them for a week before making a decision.

With lighting, ensure it is ambient and soothing. Opt for lightbulbs with rosy or peachy tones to make skin tones glow. Eyes need a break from artificial light, so try to harness natural sunlight or light candles, turning the bathroom into a soft, glowing grotto.

One of the things that makes bathing so relaxing is that it liberates the body from its own weight. Therefore, you should invest in a generously deep bath. The water should cover your shoulders and your head should be properly supported. Enhance the sensation of your skin. After bathing, freshen and awaken the body and skin with a short, cold shower—reputed to stimulate the immune system, close cleansed pores, and encourage circulation. Finish the tactile experience by drying yourself with velvety cotton towels or use waffle-textured linen towels for an additional scrub down. With thorough cleansing, the skin will tingle, and feel awakened and revitalized.

Scents calm or revive mind, body, and flagging spirits. Choose essential oils, fresh flowers, and bath oils, foams, or salts depending on your emotional and physical needs (see Scented Baths, page 83). Fragrances such as lavender and rose are calming and reassuring, while citrus-based products such as lime, lemon, and orange provide zest and energy.

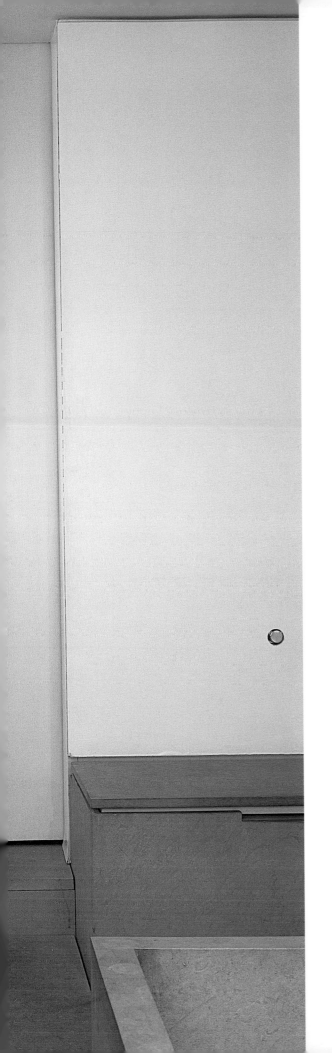

To really relax, try shutting out the sounds of the outside world. Locate your bath away from busy roads. Block out neighborhood noise with double-glazed windows and added insulation. Music is a soothing aural balm, so wire speakers into the bathroom.

In a large room, think about creating a private, fur-lined nook dedicated to post-bath repose. Here, you can rest, undertake beauty routines, receive a massage, mediate, read, or curl up catlike and simply doze. Or stretch out, cool down, and sprawl out on a daybed, chaise longue, or futon-covered bench.

To truly make the bathroom a place of peace, treat it like a sanctuary. In Scandinavian culture, the sauna is considered sacred. In the confines of its four pine walls, no heated conversations or family tiffs are permitted. It is neutral territory. Make the bathroom the home's chapel. Dedicate it solely to relaxation and rejuvenation.

Shadows are as important as light. They create an interesting effect in a space. The best-designed spaces have a great balance of both light and shadow.

Above: There's so much more to bathing than hygiene—fill a tub with soothing warm water and enjoy a soak for optimal relaxation.

Opposite: Minimalist bathrooms, like this one created by famed architect John Pawson, are completely free from the trappings of everyday life. Inspired by Japanese traditions, his design enables bathers to rinse, scrub, and cleanse their bodies before stepping into hot water and completely liberating mind, body, and spirit. To do this, the entire bathroom is a wet area—water can splash freely.

lighten **up**

MIX PRACTICALITY AND SENSUAL PLEASURE.
DIRECT NATURAL LIGHT IS THE MOST PREFERABLE
OPTION, BUT BECAUSE THE BATHROOM IS USED
EITHER LATE AT NIGHT OR EARLY IN THE MORN-
ING, ARTIFICIAL LIGHT IS UNAVOIDABLE. STILL,
YOU CAN EASILY DESIGN A SCHEME THAT WILL
ENHANCE THE BATHING EXPERIENCE.

- Safety first. Electricity and water are a potentially lethal combination, so always consult with a professional. Light fixtures must be specially designed to cope with steamy environments.

- Avoid glaring lights. Strong lighting makes a bathroom feel like an operating room and is unflattering. Avoid direct light, and instead mix up, down, and side lighting. Opt for halogen spotlights, which have a clean, white glow or recessed fluorescent strip lights for soft halos of light.

- Think function. Ensure that areas where tasks are performed are well lit, such as around the sink (for shaving and makeup). If you like to read in the bath, fit a light either above or to the side of the bath to prevent eyestrain.

- Candle, candle burning bright. Create a warm ambience by dotting the bathroom with pillars and votives.

In this space, direct lighting is provided over the in-wall mirror for activities like shaving an applying makeup. Further lighting is provided by recessed ceiling fixtures.

Opposite and above: Late afternoon light diffused through an opaque window creates a calm, placid atmosphere in this spare, urban bathing space.

Sleek pale wood cabinet faces and paneling combine with warm-toned white stone sink and bath to create a calm, soothing atmosphere.

Above: Ignite the senses with tactile surfaces, such as this black wooden bath mat, smooth soap, and coarse towel.

Left: Though tucked into a small space, this black-and-white, uncluttered bathroom manages to be a tranquil haven. A black marble surround provides a shelf for sundries: a cup of coffee, a glass of water, and a fresh towel.

SCENTED BATHS

THE ROMANS WERE GREAT ADVOCATES OF MAKING BATHING A SENSUAL AND AROMATIC EXPERIENCE. THEY EVEN COINED THE WORD LAVENDER FROM *LAVARE,* MEANING "TO WASH." AROMATHERAPISTS ADVOCATE THAT SCENTS IMPROVE OUR WELL-BEING. WHEN PLACED IN A BATH, THE SCENTS INFILTRATE THE BODY THROUGH ITS PORES; OR WHEN INHALED, THE SCENTS ARE DIFFUSED INTO THE LUNGS AND CARRIED AROUND THE BODY. ADD DROPS OF ESSEN-TIAL OILS OR MAKE YOUR OWN HERBAL INFUSION BY HANGING A MUSLIN BAG FILLED WITH FRESH OR DRIED HERBS UNDER A HOT RUNNING TAP AS THE BATH FILLS UP.

Opposite: To create a relaxing cocoon far away from the troubles of the world, designer Marja Walters has added an end wall for extra privacy.

Top and bottom: Lavender (top) is reputed to help skin heal, relax the body and strengthen the immune system, while rosemary (bottom) is a tonic for the nerves, heart, circulatory system, and digestion.

Above: Splurge on small accessories and soaps to enhace your bathroom retreat. A seashell-shaped soap pays tribute to nature.

Opposite: A bathing space design by John Pawson pays hommage to the essential elements for bathing: water and stone.

Following pages: White creates a sense of calmness and serenity. To save it from becoming too cold and clinical, this design is tempered with nature-inspired objects.

Opposite: A curved mosaic wall provides a private nook for the bather.

Right: Lighting strips illuminate this shower room, but aren't too overbearing. As most people shower usually first thing in the morning or last thing at night, the last thing they want to face is glaring lights.

heat

WET SKIN AND CHANGES IN TEMPERATURE
NEVER GO WELL TOGETHER. KEEP BATHROOMS
AMBIENT. IDEALLY, THE TEMPERATURE SHOULD
BE ABOUT 77°F (25°C).

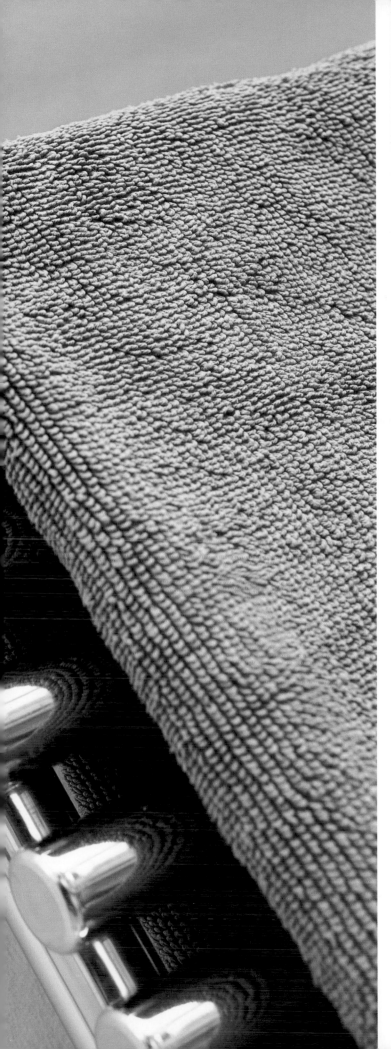

- Radiate style. Make the bathroom warm, but do it with style. Radiators, easily linked to the central heating or hot water system, are maintenance free, and come in a huge range of styles. For a retro look, salvage old radiators and give them a makeover.

- Towel rails. Heated towels are a wonderful luxury but don't rely on towel rails (unless it's a large ladder towel rail) to warm the bathroom. Supplement with a heater or wall radiator.

- Underfloor heating. Don't tread on cold tiles—install underfloor heating. The most common system is a "wet" system, which involves piping hot water beneath the floor off a central heating system. Electric floor systems are also available.

- Stoves and fireplaces. Coal burning stoves (which can also act as water heaters) and fireplaces make excellent heating options for traditional bathrooms.

Left and above: Heated towel rails provide one of life's greatest luxuries: warm towels to wrap around our cold, wet selves as we emerge from the shower.

Above: A smooth stone sink resonates with glossy modern hardware to create a tranquil setting for reflection, Zen style.

Right: Organic shapes and forms ground this minimalist-style bathroom. Stack a pile of fluffy towels to soften stark lines of such a modern space—the contrast of hard and soft materials makes the space more inviting.

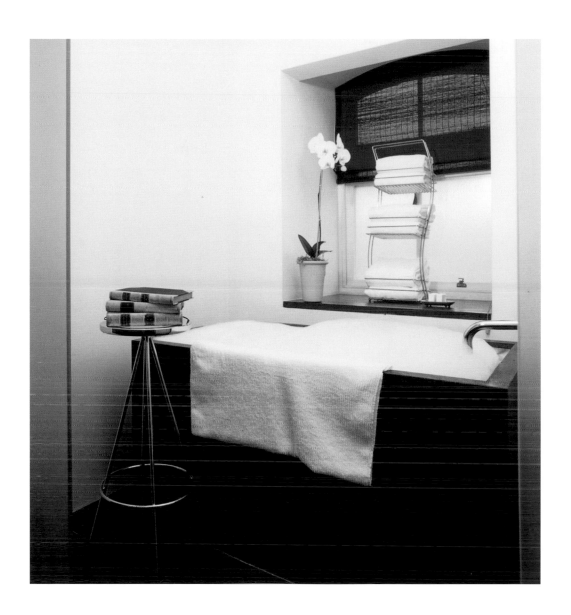

Opposite and above: A rectangular black marble bath, surrounded by precious few things: a wavy towel rack, a beautiful fragrant orchid, and a stack of books.

in harmony
with nature

THE MANTRA OF THE ECO-WARRIORS, "ACT GLOBAL, THINK LOCAL," HAS REACHED THE EARS OF INTERIOR DESIGNERS AND ARCHITECTS.

In Hindi philosophy, trees are poems the Earth creates for the heavens. In this wood-inspired interior, indoors and outdoors almost merge into one.

With ever-diminishing resources and concerns about our impact on environment, interiors now strive to work ecologically as well as functionally and aesthetically—and that includes the bathroom.

Natural interiors make sense on an emotional and spiritual level as well as on an environmental one. Recent statistics show that most Westerners spend 90 percent of their time indoors—urban life is all too often divorced from earthy pleasures. The bathroom is an ideal place to reestablish a connection with grounding, healing nature. Things like the solid feeling of warm stone underfoot, a whiff of fragrant wood, or the sight of fresh blooms act as nature's calling cards, reminding us of our intrinsic bond with the world outside our walls.

Water is a precious commodity, but the notion that a shower uses less water than a bath is a popular misconception. An average bath is filled at 8.8 to 13.2 gallons (40 to 60 l) of water, however, a power shower (where a booster pump is installed to increase water pressure) can gush an extravagant 5.5 gallons (25 l) per minute. To enjoy a shower without wasting excessive amounts of water, invest in an aerating showerhead, which will lower the flow rate to around a satisfying 1.54 gallons (7 l) per minute. Other water-saving ideas are equally as pragmatic: fix all dripping taps, and to ensure better flow control, install quarter-turn taps to stem the outflow of water.

The toilet flushes away about a third of an average household's drinking water. Find out what your local regulations require and where possible, opt for a system with a half flush.

Decorate in harmony with the environment. Ensure floors and walls are swathed in eco-friendly products. Paint walls with organic paints, based on plant oils, resins, and natural ingredients. It's worth the extra expense. Why? Their cheaper synthetic cousins create an impermeable plasticlike membrane over walls, which prevents the material underneath from ventilating. Natural paints and materials allow rooms to "breathe." Ecological floor coverings include cork, a sustainable material that's soft and warm underfoot, local stone, or natural linoleum made from powdered cork, linseed oil, wood resin, and backed with hessian.

The bathroom is the most humid room in the house. It is, therefore, a great breeding ground for fungus and mildew. Prevention, in this case, is far better than exterminating growths with toxic removers. Clay plaster on the ceiling and upper walls, regular cleaning, adequate ventilators, and a humidistat (a device that expels moist warm air when a bathroom reaches a certain humidity level), all combine to prohibit damp conditions.

Why use ersatz lemon-scented air fresheners (which contain naphthalene, phenol, and toxic chemicals) when natural ones will do? Use potpourri, scented candles, essential oils, or sweet-smelling incense sticks to refresh the air. Plants also aid in oxygenating and purifying the air. Several varieties, such as peace lilies *(Spathiphyllum),* daisies, bamboo palms, dwarf date palms, and orchids are efficient at expelling toxins. And fresh air, which comes with its own perfume (rain, sun-baked earth, or aromas caught in the breeze), is inimitable.

Summon nature indoors by creating skylights and porthole windows for views of the clouds, treetops, and birds. Or, scatter around shells and driftwood from beach walks. Bathe in water, but surround yourself in treasured booty from the Earth.

A rustic shower. A bucket filled with rainwater is attached via a pulley system to the ceiling. Everything in the bathroom (except the towels and mirrors) has been made out of local materials.

Simply natural, pared-back style. Adobe earth walls, a tented ceiling, and wooden floors create a grounded look, but the freestanding bath and Indian daybed remain the centers of attention.

a window on the **world**

WINDOWS ARE THE CRUCIAL ARCHITECTURAL
ELEMENT IN A BATHING SPACE. BESIDES
PROVIDING CRITICAL VENTILATION AND ALLOWING
CIRCULATING AIR TO DISPEL MOISTURE,
WINDOWS HARNESS NATURAL LIGHT AND INSTILL
A VITAL CONNECTION TO THE OUTSIDE WORLD.

- Maximize air and light. As bathing spaces are used early in
  the morning or late in the day, ensure windows are positioned
  to let in sunlight and air. Expand windows or punch out
  skylights. (In many neighborhoods, you don't need planning
  permission as long as the shape of the roof isn't changed;
  conservation-area inhabitants should seek advice first.)

- Add natural light to windowless rooms. A smart solution
  for boxed-in rooms is a light tube—a tubular skylight with
  a highly reflective shaft—that siphons bright daylight from
  upper levels into windowless rooms.

- Choose window coverings wisely. If you live in a built-up
  urban area, keep out prying eyes by selecting windows
  made from sandblasted or acid-etched glass. Otherwise, opt
  for window coverings such as café curtains, opaque roller
  blinds, or slatted shutters that diffuse light yet eschew
  intrusive onlookers.

- Ventilate. In the winter, windows obviously can't be relied
  upon to provide ventilation, so consider installing a ventilation fan to expel moist air. In a windowless room, this is
  mandatory.

What could create a more harmonious feeling with nature than bathroom doors
that open out onto a deck?

Above: Keep towels in wickerwork baskets, which ventilate, keeping them fresh and aired.

Left: Swathe floors in natural materials, like earthen tiles (seen here), which aid in bringing nature indoors. A rush-matting bath mat feels textural underfoot and blends in with other natural tones.

CLEAN, NOT MEAN

WHAT CIRCLES YOUR SHOWER DRAIN EVENTUALLY
ENDS UP IN THE FOOD CHAIN, SO TRY TO USE NAT-
URAL CLEANSERS SUCH AS VEGETABLE OIL
SOAPS AND HERBAL SHAMPOOS. INSTEAD OF
USING HARSH BLEACHES TO CLEAN YOUR BATH-
ROOM, TRY NATURAL DISINFECTANTS. FOR A GOOD,
GENERAL CLEANSER, A TEASPOON OF BAKING
SODA AND BORAX WITH TWO CUPS OF HOT WATER
AND A THIRD OF A CUP OF VINEGAR. APPLY WITH
A SPONGE.

Opposite: Upward growing plants placed near downwards
draining water sources stop precious chi or energy flowing out
of the house, according to feng shui philosophy.

Left: Natural fibers and oils are good for the skin. For fresh,
naturally scrubbed cells with pumice, loofahs, natural-bristled
brushes and rough-weave linen face cloths.

Following pages:
Left: The natural theme is continued in these bathing
accoutrements.

Right: Good natural architecture should always try to draw
upon the surrounding landscape. Here, the bathroom inte-
grates with the great outdoors in the Maldives.

showers

NOTHING BEATS A SHOWER FOR AN EFFICIENT, INVIGORATING WASH. A QUICK DUNK IN A JET OF WATER IS AN ESSENTIAL PICK-ME-UP FOR THOSE WITH BUSY LIVES.

• Fit a shower anywhere. Showers don't have to fit in bath-rooms. Manufacturers now make showers in watertight, self-contained units that are able to fit under redundant hall cupboards or stairwells. A second shower room helps to alleviate congestion at peak times.

• Shower surrounds. Prevent shower spray from wetting the bathroom with an effective shower screen, door, or curtain. Sliding glass screen panels are chic, practical, but also expensive. Even if the shower is fitted over the bath, some sort of screen will be necessary.

• Choose fixtures and fittings carefully. A fixed overhead rosehead looks merely aesthetic but will always provide a full deluge. For flexibility (if you want just a quick body wash, for example), a hand-held hose shower fitting is a preferable option.

• Select models with varying spray options. Modern technol-ogy has developed an array of spray jets (needle jets, relax-ing pulses, and alternating pressures). Choose one to suit your needs, or opt for a fixture with variable spray jets.

Above: Elemental style. Indoors blend with the outdoors in this all-natural bathroom in the Maldives.

Opposite: The old beams add rusticity and style to this modern bathroom. Why tear down old stuff when it can be resurrected? Recycle and repair instead of throwing away.

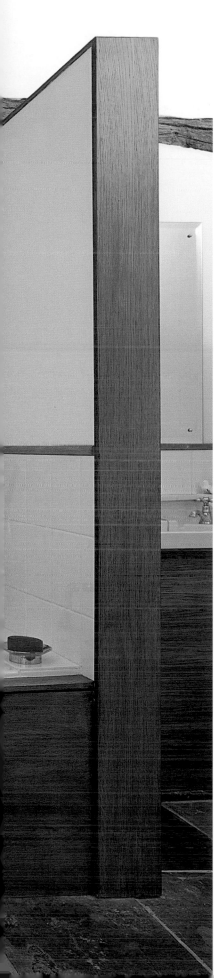

Left and above: There are many ways to bring nature into your bathing space. Fresh flowers are but one alternative. Use natural materials and include artwork with soothing nature-inspired images.

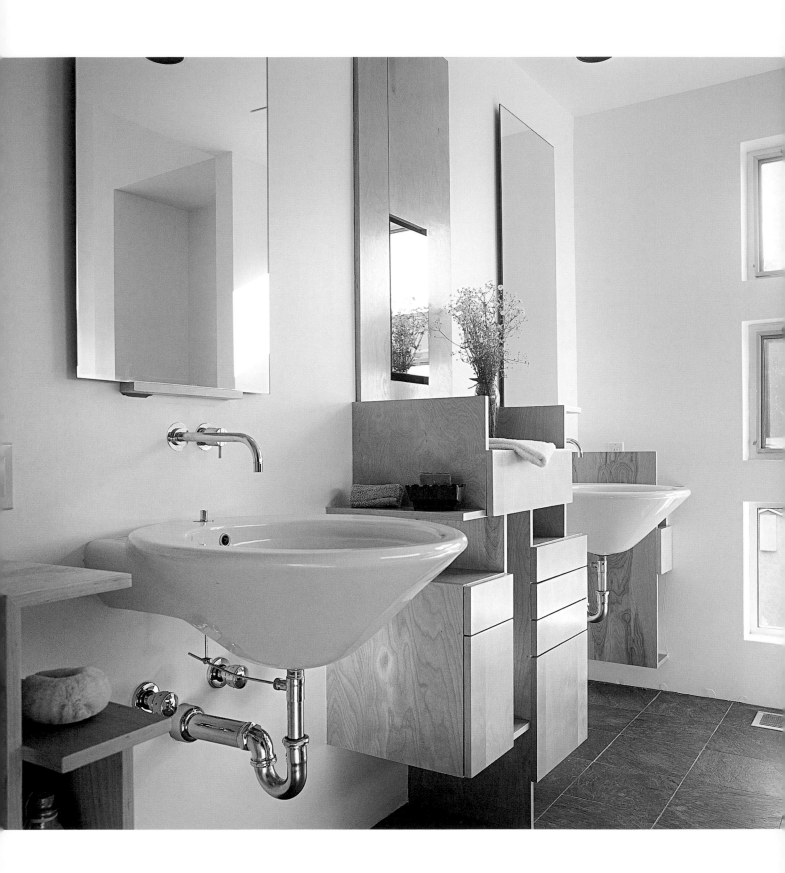

Opposite: Three windows provide a full-length view of the outside world in bite-sized chunks. In urban vistas, just a glimpse of the sky acts as nature's calling card.

Above: Slough off dead skin cells and wash with natural products.
Your skin will thank you.

Opposite: Bring nature into your bathroom. If not with flowers or plants, make a permanent display of stones, starfish, and pebbles from seaside rambles.

Above: Natural light and air bring this bathroom to life. An extra pair of wooden bath mats complements and protect the wooden floor.

Opposite: The handsome natural wood bathtub casing and cabinetry convey a nautical feeling. A slatted footboard is both an aesthetic and practical solution to stepping out of the bathtub.

Above: Creamy white porcelain contrasts beautifully with the natural wood backsplash. You can decorate with wood in the bathroom; just make sure wood is protected with several coats of polyurethane.

Following pages:
Left: Keep natural materials such as this slate floor underfoot to ground you.

Right: Naturally airy, naturally light, naturally spacious. The bathing space ideal.

exotic soaks

IMAGINE EASING YOUR TIRED BODY INTO A HOT SPA BATH

UNDER THE STARS, OR A BATHROOM THAT'S A MINI HEALTH RETREAT, OR STEPPING OUT-
SIDE INTO THE BRISK, MORNING AIR AND ENJOYING A CASCADE OF WARM RAINWATER.

A little unconventional thought, a touch of exotica, or a dose of hydrotherapy, and your bathroom can easily transform into a room that really makes a splash.

Create a mini health retreat by drawing on hydrotherapy (the use of water for medicinal purposes), championed throughout the centuries as a method of easing muscular and joint aches and pains, stimulating the circulation, and reducing stress. Health spas and springs were—and still are—used by many cultures as a physical and spiritual restorative. For centuries, inventors sought a way to emulate the massaging effect of effervescent waters, and finally, in 1966, Italian-born aircraft designer Roy Jacuzzi pioneered the eponymous spa bath.

Jacuzzi used a combination of water pressure and aerated jets of water to pummel the bather's body and revive, relax, tone, and stimulating muscles. Spa baths are reported to relieve stress, expel toxins, and increase the flow of blood to the joints and skin tissues. The range of designs available has proliferated and a number of manufacturers now produce ordinary baths that have massaging jets.

Jacuzzi's bath inspired tubs to come out of the bathroom and into the garden. Tubs take up less room than swimming pools and are easily integrated into the garden or patio's design. There are a few practical considerations, however. A standard tub measures about 5 feet by 4 feet (1.5 m x 1 m) and houses about 415 gallons (1,893 l) of water. That's already pretty heavy by itself, so ensure the site and decking is strong enough to hold the bath's weight or, dig it into the ground. Aside from the tub, you'll also need to consider drainage, the filter, pump, and a water heater. Solar panels are a great way to conserve energy (and reduce your electric bill), and for those who live in climates with sunshine for more than six hours a day, these panels provide 70 to 100 percent of heat.

An outdoor shower, oriental style. Here, the shower doesn't have an enclosure, enabling the bather to feel at one with the surrounding environment.

To securely revel in an outdoor bath or shower, ensure the site is private. Ideally, position it in a relatively shady area. Stave off winds (and prying eyes) with a row of evergreens, or bamboo, wood, or canvas screens. To prevent small children from harm, build a 4-foot (1.2 m) -high fence around the perimeter. Plant flowers such as jasmine and roses around the tub to perfume the air; for nighttime fragrances, try honeysuckle or night-scented stock.

You might try a rustic approach. Find an old bath (if the bath doesn't have legs, mount it on piles of bricks, fill it with water, and light a fire beneath it. Leave it to smolder for at least an hour until the water is piping hot. The base of the bath might be too hot to sit on, so put a log in the tub on which to sit. Then, luxuriate beneath the night sky.

Outdoor showers are equally as invigorating. For a simple shower, rig up a solar water heater and enjoy a sun-heated deluge in the open air. Most outdoor shops have sell easy-to-install systems. Again, a screen for shelter and decking to stand on ensure comfort and privacy.

Although outdoor baths are exotic places to bathe, indoor bathrooms can be equally striking. Create a bathroom theme with a twist by drawing upon other cultures or eras. Imagine where you'd most like to escape to: the plush bathroom of the Sun King in seventeenth-century France; a chapellike Zen sanctuary; a Turkish bathroom, where hand-knotted Persian rugs hang on the wall, whatever suits you. Indulge in exotic fantasies, then collect furnishings and fittings to fulfill the bathroom of your dreams.

Emulate this outdoor shower on a terrace in Manhattan by creating your own; home stores and outdoor shops offer easy-to-install shower systems.

a home **health** spa

CREATE YOUR OWN WEEKEND RETREAT. TELL
YOUR FRIENDS YOU'VE GONE ON VACATION,
THEN ENJOY LOUNGING AROUND THE
BATHROOM.

- Make your own flotation tank. Pilgrims walk miles to
  soak in the healing, salty waters of the Dead Sea. Make
  your own version. Add 1 pound (500 g) of Epsom salts,
  $1/2$ pound (250 g) of sea salt, and one dessert spoon of
  clear iodine (to prevent bath stain) to your next bath.

- Infuse your bath with fresh scents. Gather rose petals or
  pine needles or chop up lemons and oranges and put them
  in a muslin bag. Hang the bag under hot tap for about ten
  minutes while running the bath, then hop in and enjoy.

- Treat yourself to natural skin treatments. Pumice (a vol-
  canic stone), brushes with natural bristles, or loofahs
  scrub away dead skin cells. Replenish dry skin with yogurt
  mixed with fresh mint; for a natural toner, splash on your
  face a concoction of teaspoon of cider vinegar added to a
  cup of water. Runny honey is nature's moisturizer. Rub in
  with fingertips, then wash off.

Above: Before plumbing was invented, we bathed in rivers, lakes, and streams. On a basic level, bathing outdoors appeals to our primal instincts, while on a natural level it's just incredibly pleasurable to enjoy basking in water surrounded by living, breathing plants and pure fresh air.

Opposite: Create your own marriage of outdoors and indoors by rigging up an outdoor shower system in a private corner of your garden.

bathrooms with **style**

WITHOUT STYLE, BATHROOMS HAVE NO PER-
SONALITY. TAKE YOUR INSPIRATION FROM
GLOBAL CULTURE, NATURE, TECHNOLOGY, OR
BYGONE ERA. CHOOSE THE LOOK OR THEME
THAT MAGNETIZES YOU. FOLLOWING ARE JUST
A FEW SUGGESTIONS.

- Modern rustic. Mix natural materials (like wood, wicker and unbleached linens) with elemental furnishings and fittings (such as a stainless-steel bath or a glass basin). Include plants, pebbles from the beach, and natural accessories. Waterproofed wooden tubs complete the effect.

- Zen (far left). Think minimalist. Keep the palette neutral (browns, taupes, blacks, and whites) and ensure all surfaces are pared back and clutter free. Go for a rectangular tub in black marble.

- Hi tech (top left). Opt for sleek, streamlined fittings and swathe the whole room in chrome, glass, stainless steel, and mirrors. A glass or stainless-steel bath is a fitting focal point.

- Traditional (middle left). Revive stately style with sumptuous decoration and original fittings. Make the bathroom's centerpiece a large, cast-iron roll-top bath.

- Bohemian chic (bottom left). Pitch eclectic furnishings and ornaments against colorful backdrops and drape vibrant curtains around windows. An antique French bateau bath adds to the look.

DIVIDE AND RULE

DIVISIONS OF SPACE ARE DECORATIVE OR PRACTI-
CAL. SCREENS, FOR EXAMPLE, ARE A GREAT WAY
TO CREATE PRIVATE DRESSING SPACES AND TO
HANG ROBES. HOWEVER, IF THE BATHROOM IS EN
SUITE, YOU MAY WANT TO FIND A MORE DEFINI-
TIVE WAY TO SEPARATE THE TWO ROOMS, SUCH AS
WITH SLIDING GLASS DOORS, FOLDING PANELS, OR
COLORFUL BEADS HUNG FROM THE CEILING.

A modern interpretation of the Japanese outdoor pool. Here,
a folding screen leads out onto a terrace where a wooden
pool awaits.

SOURCE LIST

SUPPLIERS AND FITTINGS

Acorn Engineering Company
15125 Proctor Ave.
City of Industry, CA 91744
Tel: 800-591-9050
Fax: 626-330-8748
E-mail: info@neo-metro.com

Alternative Plans
9 Hester Road
London
SW11 4AN
Tel:00 44 (0)207 228 6460
UK outlet for chic bathroom ranges,
including Boffi, Agape and Nito.

Americh Corporation
13212 Saticoy Street
North Hollywood, CA 91605
Tel: 800-453-1463
Fax: 818-982-2764

Artistic Tile
79 Fifth Avenue
New York, NY 10003
Tel: 212-727-9331

Bed, Bath, and Beyond
650 Liberty Avenue
Union, New Jersey 07083
Tel: 908-688-0888

Bette UK
Park View
Lower Clopton
Upper Quinton
Stratford-upon-Avon
Warwickshire
CV37 8LQ
Tel: 00 44(0)178926 2626
Bath manufactures who feature Jasper
Morrison's wave-like tub

Boffi Bagni
Via Oberdan 70
20030 Lentate sul Sevso
Milan
Italy
Tel: 00 39 0362 5341
Stylish Italian bath ware

Burgess Cabinetry & Fixtures
647 Manufacturers Drive
Westland, ME 48186
Tel: 734-729-9306
Fax: 734-729-9354

C.B. Bath, Inc.
2295 NW 102 Place
Miami, FL 33172
Tel: 305-718-8898

Colourwash
165 Chamberlayne Rd
London
SW6 3JJ
Tel: 00 44 (0) 208 459 8918
Traditional and modern fittings

Czech & Speake Showroom
39C Jermyn Street
London
SW1Y 6DN
Tel: 44 (0)207 439 0126
Elegant bathroom accessories and
fittings

Dornbracht
Unit 3 Oakwood Industrial Park
Gatwick Road
Crawley
West Sussex
RH10 2AZ
www.dornbracht.com
Tel: 00 44 (0)1293 531313
Chic German fittings

Droog
DMD Parkweg 14
227 A/Voorburg
Holland
Tel: 0031 70386 4038
Inventive bathroom Dutch
designers

Duravit
Werderstrasse 36
Postfach 240
D-78123 Hornberg
Germany
www.duravit.com
Tel: 0049 78337070
Long-lasting German style

Duravit, USA Inc.
1750 Beckenridge Parkway,
Ste.500
Duluth, GA 30096
Tel: 888-387-2848
Fax: 888-387-2843
E-mail: info@usa_duravit.com

Hansgrohe and Axor
Units D1 & D2
Sandown Park Trading Estate
Royal Mills
Esher
Surrey
KT10 88BL
Tel: 00 44 (0)1372 465465
www.hansgrohe.co.uk
Top label with funky stuff from top
designers

CP Hart
Newham Terrace
Hercules Rd
London
SE1 7DR
Tel: 0044 (0)207 902 1000
Chic bathroom wares from a
number of manufacturers

Hoesch Metall
Postfach 10 04 24
D-52304 Duren
Germany
Tel: 00 49 24 22 54 0
www.hoesch.de
Baths designed by Philippe Starck and
others

Ideal Standard
The Bathroom Works
National Avenue
Kingston-upon-Hull
East Ridding
Yorkshire
HU5 4HS
www.ideal-standard.co.uk
Tel: 00 44(0)1483 346 461
Huge range of stylish ranges

John Pawson
Unit B 70-78 York Way
Kings Cross
London
N1 9AG
Tel: 00 44(0) 207 839 2929

LEFROY BROOKS
10 Leonard Street
New York, NY 10013
Tel: 212-226-2242
Fax: 212-226-3003

Linens 'n Things
6 Brighton Road
Clifton, NJ 07015
Tel: 973-778-1300

Pottery Barn
Williams-Sonoma, Inc
3250 Van Ness Avenue
San Francisco, CA 94109

Submarine
Ushida Findlay Building
1/1.8 Lanrak St
Glasgow
Scotland
G1 5PY
Tel: 00 44(0)141 243 2424
Award-winning stainless steel baths

The Water Monopoly
16/18 Lonsdale Rd
London
NW6 6RD
Tel: 00 44(0)207 624 2636
Restored and salvaged antique French
and English bath fittings

PHOTO CREDITS

ABOUT THE AUTHOR

New Zealand-born Ali Hanan is a bathing aficionado currently living in London. When not indulging her water baby alter ego, she writes on interiors for British *ELLE Decoration, Living etc, NZ House and Garden,* and *The Independent on Sunday.* She is also the author of *Modern Rustic Living,* published by Rockport Publishers.